JOHN F. KENNEDY

A Photo-Illustrated Biography
by Steve Potts

Bridgestone Books

an imprint of Capstone Press

Facts about John F. Kennedy
• John Fitzgerald Kennedy was the 35th president of the United States.
• He was the first president of the United States born in the 20th century.
• He was the first Roman Catholic to be elected president.
• He was shot and killed by Lee Harvey Oswald.

Bridgestone Books are published by Capstone Press,
151 Good Counsel Drive, P.O. Box 669, Mankato, Minnesota 56002.
www.capstonepress.com

Library of Congress Cataloging-in-Publication Data
Potts, Steve, 1956–
   John F. Kennedy, a photo-illustrated biography/by Steve Potts
   p. cm.—(Read and discover photo-illustrated biographies)
   Includes bibliographical references and index.
   Summary: A brief biography of the thirty-fifth president of the United States.
   ISBN 1-56065-454-6 (hardcover)
   ISBN 0-7368-4469-4 (paperback)
   1. Kennedy, John F. (John Fitzgerald), 1917–1963—Juvenile literature. 2. Presidents—United States—Biography—Juvenile literature. 3. Kennedy, John F. (John Fitzgerald), 1917–1963.
[1. Presidents.] I. Title. II. Series.
E842.Z9P68   1996
973.922'092—dc20   96-02586
[B]   CIP
                                                      AC

Photo credits
Archive Photos, cover, 8, 10, 14, 18, 20
Corbis-Bettman, 6
FPG International LLC, 4, 12, 16

2 3 4 5 6 06 05 04 03 02

Table of Contents

Words in **boldface** type in the text are defined in the Words to Know section in the back of this book.

Beloved President

John Fitzgerald Kennedy remains one of the United States' most beloved leaders. President Kennedy was killed when he was young. He was mourned by people throughout the world.

John Kennedy and his wife, Jackie, brought a sense of style to Washington, D.C. Americans loved the couple and their two young children.

President Kennedy is remembered for many accomplishments. He created the Peace Corps. He fought to win civil rights for African Americans. He supported the space program. He helped improve the lives of the poor and the old.

He was only in the White House for a few years. But he left his mark on America.

John was born on May 29, 1917, in Brookline, Massachusetts, a suburb of Boston. John's parents were Joseph Kennedy and Rose Fitzgerald Kennedy. They were both grandchildren of Irish immigrants.

John and Jackie Kennedy loved to sail.

John's Family

John was one of nine Kennedy children. He was the second oldest. His father, Joseph Kennedy, was a banker, businessman, and movie producer. His mother, Rose, stayed at home to raise their children.

The Kennedys were an active family. With 11 people in the house, someone was always busy. The children took swimming, sailing, and tennis lessons.

John liked to play with his brothers and sisters. And he loved to read. His older brother, Joe, liked to tease John. As they grew up, they challenged each other in school and sports. John had two younger brothers, Bobby and Ted. They would follow in John's footsteps to serve in the U.S. Senate. Bobby was **assassinated** in 1968. He was shot and killed in California. He was running for president.

John had five younger sisters. They were Rosemary, Kathleen, Eunice, Patricia, and Jean.

Rose Kennedy poses with five of her children in 1922. They are, from left, Eunice, Kathleen, Rosemary, in front, John and Joe Jr.

School Years

John started kindergarten when he was four. He enjoyed playing with other children. He was not always a good student. He was often sick. In 1919, when he was just two, John got scarlet fever. Many children died from the disease. John got better. But for the rest of his life, he had problems with his health.

In 1931, John went to Choate School in Connecticut. John liked history and science courses. He did not like mathematics and spelling. He was active in sports. The teachers knew John liked to play tricks on his friends and break the rules.

When he was 19, John enrolled at Harvard University. He studied **politics**. In his last year of college, he wrote a long paper. It became the book *Why England Slept*. Not many college students had written a book. The book sold many copies and made John a famous young man. He later wrote another book that won the Pulitzer Prize. It was called *Profiles in Courage*.

John's book, Why England Slept, sold many copies.

War Hero

On December 7, 1941, Japan attacked the United States Navy at Pearl Harbor. America was now involved in World War II. Even though John had troubles with his back, he joined the navy. He was given command of a **PT boat**. Men on these small boats rescued American pilots and sailors in the Pacific Ocean. They also spied on the Japanese.

In August 1943, a Japanese ship rammed John's PT boat. It cut the boat in half. John helped his men swim to an island. He towed an injured sailor. Later, John swam through the ocean to other islands to get help.

After he rescued his men, John became a hero. His picture appeared in newspapers and his story was told in many magazines. Readers were amazed at what the young sailor had done. His actions to save his men made John famous

But this time was not all happy for John and his family. John's brother Joe was killed during the war.

John's brother Joe Jr., right, was killed during World War II.

House and Senate

When the war ended in 1945, John returned to Massachusetts. His father suggested he run for a seat in the U.S. Congress. John was interested in politics and thought he could win.

He ran for a seat in the House of Representatives. His family was a big help. His mother and sisters served coffee and tea to thousands of people. His brothers passed out buttons and pictures. John was a popular **candidate** for the Democratic Party. He was a handsome young war hero. John won the election.

For the next 14 years, John served in the House and then in the Senate. He helped make laws affecting education, labor unions, the military, and America's friendships with other countries. He liked helping people. While he was in the Senate, John married Jacqueline Bouvier. She was well educated and came from a well-known family. Jackie was a private person. The couple had two children, Caroline and John Jr.

Caroline Kennedy rests on her father's shoulder.

Running for President

John liked what he was doing in the Senate. But he wanted to do more. In 1960, he announced he wanted to be president.

Elections are held in November. Before that, candidates have to travel all around the country. They make many speeches and meet thousands of people.

John **debated** his Republican rival, Richard Nixon. Their debates were the first shown on television. Nixon did not come across well on television. The bright lights in the studio made him look sick. John looked energetic and handsome.

Many Americans had trouble deciding who was the better candidate. The election was very close. Nearly 69 million votes were cast. John won by just 120,000 votes.

John Kennedy became the first Roman Catholic to be elected president. At 43 years old, he was the youngest president ever elected.

John Kennedy campaigns in 1960 in Los Angeles.

Mr. President

The United States was going through changing times. John made many tough decisions while he was president.

African Americans were trying to win equal rights. Martin Luther King Jr. led marches and gave speeches. He tried to show Americans how badly his people were being treated. John had to send the National Guard to the South. They protected black students who were attending southern universities for the first time.

John's plan was called the New Frontier. He wanted to help students and the elderly. He wanted to improve the tax system. But many of his plans did not go through Congress.

John wanted to help other countries improve life for their people, too. He founded an organization called the Peace Corps. Many young Americans joined. Peace Corps workers went to Africa, Asia, and Latin America. They helped people improve their health, grow more crops, and learn to read. People around the world came to love President Kennedy because he tried to help them.

John Kennedy made many tough decisions while he was president.

United States versus the Soviet Union

The United States was competing with the Soviet Union in many ways. The Soviets sent the first astronaut into space in April 1961. John was afraid they would beat the Americans to the moon. He backed the U.S. space program. In May 1961, the first American astronaut rocketed into space. Americans were the first to reach the moon in 1969.

The Soviets and Americans were also at odds in Berlin. It was a divided city in Germany. The Soviets controlled East Berlin. They built a wall to keep people from escaping to the West. When the Soviets threatened West Berlin with a war, John visited the city. In a famous speech, he promised to protect the German people.

John had to protect the American people, too. He wanted the Soviets to take their missiles out of Cuba. This island is only 90 miles from Florida. The missiles were aimed at the United States. In 1961, an **invasion** by Cuban exiles failed. The next year, the Soviets and Americans came close to war. In the end, the two sides talked. The missiles were removed.

President Kennedy met with Soviet Premier Nikita Khrushchev.

The President Is Killed

On November 22, 1963, John traveled to Dallas, Texas. His wife, Jackie, traveled with him. As they rode in a car through the city, Lee Harvey Oswald hid on the sixth floor of the Texas Book Depository building. As the car came near the building, Oswald took aim and fired a rifle. The shots hit the president. Within the hour, John died. He was only 46.

The U.S. government said Oswald acted alone. But many people think others were involved in the assassination. It is still a mystery.

People around the world cried when John died. They wondered what he might have done if he had lived longer.

John is buried at Arlington National Cemetery in Virginia. It is just across the river from Washington, D.C. Near him are the bodies of his wife, Jackie, who died in 1994, and his brother, Bobby. An eternal flame marks the graves.

Long after his death, President Kennedy's ideas live on. He is remembered as a man who tried to help the American people lead better lives.

Lyndon B. Johnson takes the oath of office aboard Air Force One. He is standing between his wife, Lady Bird, and Jackie Kennedy.

Words from John F. Kennedy

"My fellow Americans, ask not what your country can do for you, ask what you can do for your country. My fellow citizens of the world, ask not what America will do for you, but what together we can do for the freedom of man."

From Kennedy's inaugural address,

January 20, 1961

"One hundred years of delay have passed since President Lincoln freed the slaves, yet their heirs, their grandsons, are not fully free. They are not yet freed from the bonds of injustice, they are not yet freed from social and economic oppression. And this nation, for all its hopes and all its boasts, will not be fully free until all its citizens are free."

From Kennedy's television address to the nation before sending a civil rights bill to Congress,

June 1963

Important Dates in John F. Kennedy's Life

1917—Born on May 29 in Brookline, Massachusetts

1936—Enters Harvard University

1940—Publishes his first book, *Why England Slept*

1943—PT-109 is sunk by the Japanese

1946—Elected to U.S. House of Representatives

1952—Elected to U.S. Senate

1953—Marries Jacqueline Bouvier

1957—Wins Pulitzer Prize for his book, *Profiles in Courage*

1957—Daughter Caroline born

1958—Re-elected to Senate

1960—Elected president

1960—Son John born

1961—Creates Peace Corps; tries to invade Cuba at the Bay of Pigs

1962—Forces missiles to be removed from Cuba

1963—Visits Ireland and Germany; killed in Dallas, Texas

Words to Know

assassinate—to murder by surprise attack

candidate—person who seeks office

debate—to discuss both sides of an issue

invasion—an entering by an attacking military force

politics—the art or science of governing

PT boat—small fast patrol boat, usually armed with torpedoes and machine guns

Read More

Joseph, Paul. *John F. Kennedy.* United States Presidents. Minneapolis: Abdo & Daughters, 2000.

Spies, Karen Bornemann. *John. F Kennedy.* United States Presidents. Berkeley Heights, NJ: Enslow Publishers, 1999.

Uschan, Michael V. *John F. Kennedy.* The Importance Of. San Diego: Lucent Books, 1999.

White, Nancy Bean. *Meet John F. Kennedy.* A Bullseye Biography. New York: Random House, 1993.

Useful Addresses and Internet Sites

FactHound offers a safe, fun way to find Internet sites related to this book. All of the sites on FactHound have been researched by our staff.

Here's how:
1. Visit www.facthound.com
2. Type in this special code **1560654546** for age-appropriate sites. Or enter a search word related to this book for a more general search.
3. Click on the **Fetch It** button.

FactHound will fetch the best sites for you!

Index